RUDOLF STEINER'S PATH OF INITIATION AND THE MYSTERY OF THE EGO

and

THE FOUNDATIONS OF ANTHROPOSOPHICAL METHODOLOGY

Two lectures in Bologna: on 31 March 2011 during the International Conference to mark the Centenary of Rudolf Steiner's Lecture in Bologna, and on 8 April 1911 at the Fourth International Philosophy Congress

Rudolf Steiner • Sergei O. Prokofieff

TEMPLE LODGE

Temple Lodge Publishing
Hillside House, The Square
Forest Row, RH18 5ES

www.templelodge.com

Published by Temple Lodge 2013

The lecture by Sergei O. Prokofieff was originally published in German under the title *Der Einweihungsweg Rudolf Steiners und das Geheimnis des Ich: Ein Beitrag zum Bologna-Vortrag Rudolf Steiners* by Verlag am Goetheanum, Dornach, 2011. The lecture by Rudolf Steiner (from the German GA volume 35) was previously published in *Esoteric Development*, SteinerBooks 1982

Lecture by Sergei O. Prokofieff translated by Willoughby Ann Walshe with revisions by Thomas O'Keefe, and extensively revised by Simon Blaxland-de Lange. Lecture by Rudolf Steiner translated by Olin D. Wannamaker

A catalogue record for this book is available from the British Library

ISBN 978 1 906999 55 1

Cover by Morgan Creative featuring a detail from the cupola of the first Goetheanum
Typeset by DP Photosetting, Neath, West Glamorgan
Printed and bound by Berforts Ltd., Herts.

RUDOLF STEINER (1861–1925) called his spiritual philosophy 'anthroposophy', meaning 'wisdom of the human being'. As a highly developed seer, he based his work on direct knowledge and perception of spiritual dimensions. He initiated a modern and universal 'science of spirit', accessible to anyone willing to exercise clear and unprejudiced thinking. From his spiritual investigations Steiner provided suggestions for the renewal of many activities, including education (both general and special), agriculture, medicine, economics, architecture, science, philosophy, religion and the arts. Today there are thousands of schools, clinics, farms and other organizations involved in practical work based on his principles. His many published works feature his research into the spiritual nature of the human being, the evolution of the world and humanity, and methods of personal development. Steiner wrote some 30 books and delivered over 6000 lectures across Europe. In 1924 he founded the General Anthroposophical Society, which today has branches throughout the world.

SERGEI O. PROKOFIEFF, born in Moscow in 1954, studied fine arts and painting at the Moscow School of Art. He encountered anthroposophy in his youth, and soon made the decision to devote his life to it. He has been active as an author and lecturer since 1982, and in 1991 he co-founded the Anthroposophical Society in Russia. In Easter 2001 he became a member of the Executive Council of the General Anthroposophical Society in Dornach. He is the author of numerous books available in many languages throughout the world.

Also by Sergei O. Prokofieff:

Anthroposophy and The Philosophy of Freedom
The Appearance of Christ in the Etheric
The Creative Power of Anthroposophical Christology (with Peter Selg)
Crisis in the Anthroposophical Society and Pathways to the Future (with Peter Selg)
The Cycle of the Seasons and the Seven Liberal Arts
The Cycle of the Year as a Path of Initiation
The East in the Light of the West, Parts One to Three
The Encounter with Evil and its Overcoming through Spiritual Science
The Esoteric Significance of Spiritual Work in Anthroposophical Groups
Eternal Individuality, Towards a Karmic Biography of Novalis
The Foundation Stone Meditation
The Guardian of the Threshold and The Philosophy of Freedom
The Heavenly Sophia and the Living Being Anthroposophia
May Human Beings Hear it!
The Mystery of John the Baptist and John the Evangelist
The Mystery of the Resurrection in the Light of Anthroposophy
The Occult Significance of Forgiveness
Prophecy of the Russian Epic
Relating to Rudolf Steiner
Rudolf Steiner and the Founding of the New Mysteries
Rudolf Steiner's Research into Karma and the Mission of the Anthroposophical Society
Rudolf Steiner's Sculptural Group
The Spiritual Origins of Eastern Europe and the Future Mysteries of the Holy Grail
The Twelve Holy Nights and the Spiritual Hierarchies
What is Anthroposophy?
Why Become a Member of the Anthroposophical Society?
Why Become a Member of the School of Spiritual Science?
The Whitsun Impulse

The Case of Valentin Tomberg
Valentin Tomberg, Rudolf Steiner and Anthroposophy

Contents

Foreword

A special conference—organized by the Anthroposophical Society in Italy—took place in Bologna from 31 March to 3 April, 2011. It marked the 100th anniversary of the so-called Bologna lecture, which was the only one Rudolf Steiner gave in his entire life before a philosophically trained audience.

To commemorate this event, over 900 anthroposophists and people interested in the theme of the Bologna lecture assembled in the large auditorium (a former church) at the University of Bologna, the oldest university in the world.

The very number of the participants, most of whom were from Italy but included representatives from various European and North American countries, marked this as an important event in Italian anthroposophical life.

During the conference several speakers from different parts of the world contributed to clarifying and deepening certain aspects of the Bologna lecture. Two things concerning the destiny of this unique lecture by Rudolf Steiner were given particular prominence. One was the distressing fact that his pioneering disclosures met with no real understanding among the listeners at that time (a situation which has hardly changed in the world to date). At the same time it was also strongly emphasized that the themes touched upon in the lecture have lost none of their pertinence in the succeeding years but have become even more burningly relevant because of discoveries made since it was given, especially in the areas of psychology and brain research.

Thus this lecture presents a fully valid answer to a question with which the sciences referred to are still strongly preoccupied—that of the mystery of human consciousness and its emergence within man. This is the problem with which one is faced when trying to solve the riddle of human nature. For what really distinguishes man from all other creatures of nature is—to express it specifically in Rudolf Steiner's terminology—his ego consciousness or the fact that the individual ego forms the centre of his being and thus places him at the pinnacle of the entire natural order.

In his Bologna lecture, Rudolf Steiner not only indicates the solution to this most important riddle but also describes the practical path on which every person who freely undergoes a certain inner training can find the solution himself and, moreover, not merely theoretically or philosophically but in the inner experience of his own being, by understanding and becoming conscious of his individual ego. For the answer to countless questions and riddles of human nature lies in becoming aware of this innermost aspect of man's being.

So in this lecture the reader finds a concise description of the spiritual–scientific theory of knowledge and at the same time a short outline of the anthroposophical path of schooling, on which the fundamental ideas inherent in this theory of knowledge are so transformed through inner activity that one can inwardly experience how questions that still appear insoluble at one level of consciousness can find their solution when a person reaches a higher level of consciousness through his further inner development.

In this way what was perhaps the most important thesis of the entire lecture was placed in the foreground: the possibility and, indeed, the necessity of unfolding and expanding human cognitive forces, through which alone a satisfactory solution can be found to most of life's questions as well as to the fundamental riddle that man himself represents as an ego being.

In my contribution at this congress, which took place on the evening of the first day, I had a two-fold task, in that in 2011 not only *one*, but *two* anniversaries were being celebrated at the same time: the 100th anniversary of the Bologna lecture and the 150th anniversary of Rudolf Steiner's birth. Both of these themes needed to be combined in my lecture, in that on the one hand I described how in the Bologna lecture the essential foundations are already contained for a new 'science of the human ego', which Rudolf Steiner had touched upon earlier but developed mainly in several of his later works.

On the other hand—and no less important—Rudolf Steiner was the first who not only substantiated this new scientific direction theoretically but also transformed it into a practical path, which he himself followed to its end. Therefore, all perceptions pertaining to the human ego originated from Rudolf Steiner's own inner experience, behind which was a development filled with a challenging quest for knowledge which he described as the appropriate path for present-day people to reach the spiritual world, where the true human ego originates.

In this way Rudolf Steiner built a bridge which brought his theory of knowledge, which was already established before his early philosophical works, into an inseparable union with the later anthroposophy as modern spiritual science. This transition was described most succinctly and convincingly in the Bologna lecture.[1]

As a supplement to the present text, the reader will find in this book both summaries of essential points from the lecture in which some of the thoughts in the Bologna lecture were taken further and connected with further aspects of anthroposophy, especially in relation to their Christological foundations. Inasmuch as these viewpoints are important for my remarks, both of these commentaries are included in this publication.

Finally, I want to express special thanks to the interpreter of my lecture at the Bologna congress—the anthroposophical doctor Dr Giancarlo Buccheri. Without his excellent translation and inner support I would hardly have dared to present the complex content to such a large and differentiated audience. The completely positive reaction of the congress participants to my lecture is due not only to the speaker but also to his interpreter.

I have revised the written version of the lecture for publication in German and expanded it slightly with a few further aspects regarding the theme, which could not be expressed in Bologna due to time limitations.

Goetheanum, Michaelmas 2011
Sergei O. Prokofieff

Part I

Sergei O. Prokofieff

RUDOLF STEINER'S PATH OF INITIATION AND THE MYSTERY OF THE EGO

Lecture held in Bologna on 31 March 2011 during the International Conference to mark the Centenary of Rudolf Steiner's Lecture in Bologna

Today, after 100 years, we commemorate the lecture Rudolf Steiner held here in Bologna on 8 April 1911, at the 4th Philosophical Congress. Although it is wonderful to think that this lecture took place then, this fact is also associated with a certain sadness.

Although Rudolf Steiner was undoubtedly one of the best thinkers in Europe, in his entire life he spoke only at one public philosophical congress. This happened, however, not in his native land, that is, in Austria or Germany, the countries we typically connect with the home of philosophy—he didn't appear there. But he came here to Italy, to Bologna. Now 100 years later, one can be filled with abundant thankfulness for this congress in Italy; for to it we owe this unique lecture by Rudolf Steiner.

If one now studies this lecture more extensively, one can on the one hand marvel how far Rudolf Steiner went in describing anthroposophical truths and the anthroposophical path of schooling to this audience, and on the other hand be astonished at how many anthroposophical mysteries he alluded to so clearly at the same time.

Similarly we know that at the core of this lecture there are questions which still today, 100 years later, continue to be of central scientific concern.

—How does human consciousness arise?
—What is the nature of man?
—Where is the core of man's being, his ego, to be found?

If we study this lecture by Rudolf Steiner in more detail, we will find that the central theme is the problem of the ego, which is actually located outside the body and during normal life appears in it only as a mirror image. It turns out that there are three forms of ego experience involved here: first, the image of the ego, which we connect with our normal ego consciousness; then the 'transcendental ego' as the higher ego, which exists outside the body; and finally a third even more comprehensive ego reality, which is referred to in the lecture as the 'world-ego'. Therefore, in this lecture we can speak of three ego realities.

Two years later, Rudolf Steiner described the problem of the three egos of man much more extensively in his book *The Threshold of the Spiritual World*. Here he speaks of the earthly ego; the second, higher or other ego; and the third, highest level, which he calls the true ego.

When we look at these three egos from the anthroposophical viewpoint, we can say: in the earthly ego we collect those experiences which we process and transform with the higher ego between death and a new birth. We know that in his lecture here in Bologna Rudolf Steiner also mentioned reincarnation in connection with this second, transcendental ego; for in the second or higher ego we transform the experiences collected on earth into new capacities for the next earthly life. Through this there comes about a continuation, a development from one incarnation to the next. We climb higher, the path goes ever further. But where does this path lead? Do we have a goal? Do we perhaps have a model towards which we are striving?

The answer to these questions is given to us by the world-ego, man's true ego, which now emerges as our goal. It stands before us as the highest model of a human being towards which we can aspire.

⋆

Now let us look at how Rudolf Steiner actually indicated the path through these three egos here in Bologna. He begins his lecture with a fundamental statement about the theory of knowledge, which addresses both knowledge itself and its possibilities for development. In his description, Rudolf Steiner postulates that there are different levels of human consciousness corresponding to ascending stages of knowledge. We find here the epistemological foundations of the entire path, which is described in this lecture as the path to the third, true human ego. The individual goes through a process of self-development, whereby knowledge no longer appears separated from him; and man becomes a cognitive being who is continually transforming himself, in order to overcome the limits initially established for him by nature.

Thus right at the beginning of this lecture several anthroposophical exercises are described, and there is naturally also a reference to Goethe with his archetypal plant. Goethe arrived at a symbolic image, as Rudolf Steiner called it. This is an experience that one can have on the path to the second, transcendental ego, on the path to experiencing the higher ego outside the body.

On the basis of the exercises—where one works meditatively with different symbolic pictures—that Rudolf Steiner presented in the Bologna lecture (and many more can be found in his other works), we can take the first steps in our consciousness which lead us to experience our own being outside the body. We are now achieving the first stage of supersensible consciousness. In anthroposophy it is called the imaginative stage, or that which pertains to *Imagination*. Here one is living and weaving in pictures. One experiences oneself as in the stream of time, in processes of continual metamorphosis, in the growth and the dying of nature. One lives together with nature as Goethe did with his archetypal plant.

At the same time, one lives in the purified processes of one's own thinking. When one has achieved this stage of higher knowledge, one can experience for oneself the awareness that the real being of man lives outside the body. Thus we learn that the ego consciousness otherwise experienced as the everyday ego is only a mirror image of this higher ego in the body.

However, this path of seeking the transcendental human ego goes further. We now no longer concentrate on the content of the symbolic pictures with which we have previously worked meditatively but must voluntarily extinguish them again and then concentrate only on the pure power of consciousness necessary to engender these pictures within us. In other words: one directs one's attention to the inner activity itself which unfolds behind the thought pictures. In this way we create a free space within the soul into which the spiritual world can flow. This is the next step on the path to a knowledge of higher worlds. In his writings and lectures, Rudolf Steiner calls this stage of knowledge *Inspiration*.

One now begins to observe oneself through one's own inner activity. This is the path on which the true human ego outside the body can actually be grasped. One perceives oneself in one's essential nature, thus yielding a definite experience of one's own consciousness outside one's body. By continuing the corresponding exercises on this path, one is able to grasp the nature of one's own ego consciously. In other writings, Rudolf Steiner designates this second ego as the higher human ego.

The path that has been begun now leads still further, and the next step is exceptionally difficult. It is surprising that Rudolf Steiner developed this theme in such detail during a public lecture. Essentially, he says that the experience of the higher self must now be extinguished. A person is required to eliminate from his consciousness all the inner experience of living and weaving in his own self that he has achieved with so much effort. He must voluntarily eliminate the self that has been arrived at with such effort. This brings him to the next, higher stage of supersensible consciousness. Rudolf Steiner calls it the stage of *Intuition*.

The word 'Intuition' should be understood in the way Rudolf Steiner uses it, and not as it is otherwise used in philosophy or normal life. For here we are talking about the highest stage of spiritual knowledge, which we have now achieved.

At this stage we are drawing close to what in the Bologna lecture Rudolf Steiner calls the world ego. It is connected with what he describes as the third or true human ego. Here we meet something quite mysterious in the human being on the path of schooling. For what does it really mean for the human ego to flow together with the world ego without losing the individual ego being? In this regard, I would like to read aloud a passage from the Bologna lecture and from the summary of his lecture that Rudolf Steiner drafted.

In the lecture itself the next goal of the path is described and formulated as follows: 'Spiritual research would then be conceived as the way by which one attains knowledge of the real nature of that which is reflected.' In accordance with the concept of three egos, this means that a person must initially come to a conscious connection with the second, higher ego. It is the intermediate station on the path leading from the earthly ego via the higher ego to the true ego.

Then in his summary Rudolf Steiner poses the following question: Does theosophy contradict Christianity? Is it, as is often maintained, a type of neo-Buddhism? His unequivocal answer is: No! Why? Because in the Bologna lecture he is speaking not about traditional theosophy but about pure anthroposophy, which has the human being, anthropos, at its centre. This embodies the mystery of the human ego in connection with the whole world, with the cosmos. Furthermore, anthroposophy (in contrast to the entire theosophical movement) rests on the solid epistemological foundation which Rudolf Steiner developed in his early philosophical works.

Rudolf Steiner asks a further question in his summary: What is the relation of the spiritual researcher as characterized in the lecture to the Christ Being? His answer is: 'The epitome of supersensible observation consists of the fact that in the spiritual world Christ is recognized as the guiding force.' Immediately after this, Rudolf Steiner becomes even more specific: 'The more the soul develops supersensible cognitive powers, the nearer it comes to the Christ Being.'

If we now connect these words with those from the Bologna lecture, we have two different lines of thought that converge in their objective. The first is the search for the human ego, for its true nature. This path covers three stages: from the earthly ego to the higher ego and then to the true ego. This is at the same time the path to supersensible knowledge.

What happens, however, when we proceed consistently along this path? We then come ever closer to the Christ Being. On the basis of Rudolf Steiner's words cited above, the following picture emerges: what is happening is that two creative elements are meeting in a third, the true human ego. What is coming together here? The true human being, the true ego, is meeting the Christ Being. In anthroposophy, the Christ Being is related to the human ego; for in the spiritual world, Christ represents the principle of the ego as its highest example and also its eternal archetype. Here they converge: the human soul developing upward from below and Christ, who mercifully inclines towards it from the heights.

Naturally, in man we are only concerned with the microcosmic human ego. With Christ we have to do with the world ego, the comprehensive divine ego. Nevertheless, there is a mysterious connection between the human ego and Christ's world ego. In one place in his works, Rudolf Steiner asks: What is the esoteric name of Christ? He answers: His real name is 'I am.'

When we come across the word 'I am' seven times in the Gospel of John (for example: I am the way, the truth and the life), then instead of representing a grammatical form these words 'I am' indicate the esoteric name of Christ Himself. His esoteric name is: I am. Rudolf Steiner summarizes this mystery by saying: 'The only true name of Christ is "I am": Whoever doesn't know and understand that and calls Him something else doesn't know anything at all about Him. "I am" is His only name.'[2]

This results in a quite new perspective of Christianity, which comes about from a new relationship of the human being to Christ. In other words, if we follow the path outlined by Rudolf Steiner in the Bologna lecture—which leads to the highest aspect of the human ego—sufficiently far, that is, if we seek and find our deepest human nature, we also thereby encounter Christ. He is the greatest model of this development which is inherently possible—and will ever be possible—for man; the highest goal to which we as human beings are able to aspire.

We want it not only because we are or want to be Christians, but because we are *human beings*; because every person possesses an ego.

Whether Christian, Muslim, or Buddhist, everyone is in the first instance a human being with an individual ego that is reflected in the body and yet can only be found outside the body. Furthermore, there is also a third ego that we cherish as the highest ideal of mankind's development, in which Christ is present in every person.

Now we understand why Christ in His essential Being belongs not only to Christians, as is often thought, but to *all* people, because they are all ego beings. Each person is following the path to Christ in so far as he has begun the journey to the source of his own being. It was this journey which, in his Bologna lecture, Rudolf Steiner described as the suitable path of schooling for the present-day. It is the modern path to Christ.

When we reach the end of the path after many earthly incarnations, we will not only know but also really experience how the human ego is related in its highest aspect to Christ.[3]

Modern spiritual science makes us aware how Christ is connected with the true human ego as its highest model and archetype. However, it is only since the Mystery of Golgotha, when Christ united Himself with the whole evolution of the Earth, that He can also be found in each true human ego.

★

After having considered the Bologna lecture in the framework of this great Christological perspective of anthroposophy, now let us attempt—if only aphoristically—to say something about the second theme of this evening's lecture: Where is this spiritual path which is described in the Bologna lecture to be found in Rudolf Steiner's life? For the path to the true human ego which Rudolf Steiner describes in this lecture is one that he himself followed. It is only because he followed the path himself that he could give this lecture—and bring all of anthroposophy to the world. Thus a few important points in Rudolf Steiner's life should be presented briefly here.

There are pre-eminently two sources available for this study: on the one hand, Rudolf Steiner's autobiographical lecture from 1913—and his autobiography, which he published at the end of his life. From these two sources we know that when he was a seven-year-old boy Rudolf Steiner discovered he had certain clairvoyant faculties. In themselves, however, these were nothing unusual. At this time, especially in secluded rural regions of Europe, it was quite usual for children to possess certain visionary faculties. However, what basically differentiated Rudolf Steiner in his early childhood from others who had similar abilities was something else.

When Rudolf Steiner was eight years old, his family moved to Neudörfl, a larger town where he also attended school. There he soon discovered geometry. This discovery became a formative experience for his entire life. Naturally, as a child, Rudolf Steiner could not yet formulate what I am saying now. However, he reports that already then, at this youthful age, the following mood lived in him: one must let all spiritual perceptions live within oneself just as in geometry;[4] for in geometry we do not merely behold the spirit but can also think clearly about it.

What do we do, for instance, when we think of an ideal circle? We think about something that no person can ever perceive with his physical senses. With our eyes we perceive only innumerable variations of a circle; we can call forth the ideal circle only in the course of a pure spiritual activity in our soul.

Here we find a direct connection with the second part of the Bologna lecture, where mathematics is mentioned as an activity of the human ego outside the body. And the most impressive thing about this experience of Rudolf Steiner's is that as an eight-and-one-half-year-old boy he already envisioned before him his whole life's task, that task which led him later to found spiritual science, which is concerned with the connection of spiritual impressions with clear, scientific thinking. That was something totally new in the whole of mankind's evolution.

For in the course of mankind's history there have always been clairvoyant personalities who can see into the spiritual world. Such great individuals can be found in all religions. Rudolf Steiner, however, had a quite specific task placed before him: How can a person combine clairvoyance with clear, scientific thinking? He was the first person who could completely accomplish this task.

At this point we must ask the question: Why combine clairvoyance with thinking, why not with feeling or willing? The reason is obvious and directly connected with the subject of the ego, with the quest for the ego, which of course is our theme here. The answer is: It is only in thinking that we are completely awake as ego beings. Only in thinking does our ego consciousness develop to its full extent. In feeling we are in a dreamlike condition. In willing we live in deep, dreamless sleep consciousness.

What happens when I move something in the outer world through my will forces, for example, this watch on my lectern, what happens then? At first I form a clear idea of what I want to do, and then observe how my hand carries out this movement. I have, however, no idea how my ideal idea is transformed into a practical deed and my hand is set into movement through the will. That is the reason why today we can be perfectly awake, modern human beings only in thinking.

Our current civilization is born out of thinking, because we experience ourselves in thinking as fully conscious ego beings and can only grasp our freedom through it. We become independent and self-determining beings only in thinking. This is what Rudolf Steiner describes in his early work *The Philosophy of Spiritual Activity (The Philosophy of Freedom)*, where he also establishes this entire process scientifically and philosophically.

★

In one of his anthroposophical lectures, Rudolf Steiner speaks about three stages of thinking.[5] These have a certain parallel to what is also brought out in the Bologna lecture. The first stage consists of the intellectual thinking we possess without exception, for the simple reason that we belong to the current civilization. This thinking is linked to our body and its sense perceptions. Then there is a second type of thinking, which Rudolf Steiner also calls morphological thinking and links directly with Goethe. A wonderful example of this morphological thinking is Goethe's archetypal plant. It is a thinking which works inwardly not with facts but with processes that grow and thrive as well as wilt and die, like a plant. This thinking resides in the living stream of time rather than in spatial ideas. Rudolf Steiner indicated that it was out of this thinking that he wrote his *Philosophy of Spiritual Activity*. That was also the reason why this book could not be easily understood at that time. For one simply cannot grasp it with intellectual thinking.

Rudolf Steiner also stated that the wonderful, flowing forms of the first Goetheanum emerged from this morphological thinking,[6] which is why he named this building the *Goetheanum*.

Then there is still a third type of thinking. How does one now achieve this kind of thinking, which can alone be taken into the spiritual world and enable full human ego consciousness to be maintained there? In order to understand this, we can consider the important passage in *The Philosophy of Spiritual Activity* where Rudolf Steiner speaks about the 'exceptional state'. Here too we can also find a parallel to the Bologna lecture. How is this exceptional state produced in thinking?

Although Hegel, in his time, was already on the road to realizing this goal, he got stuck in a more theoretical approach. He was convinced that a person could understand and explain everything in the world with thinking. And after thinking had elucidated everything, what more was there for it to do? Now it had to account for itself, had to describe how it functions. Therefore, for Hegel the epitome of the entire body of knowledge was the composing of a *Logic*. And he wrote a book—a really thick book—with precisely this title.

But Aristotle, not Hegel, was the father of logic. Rudolf Steiner forms a connection with *this* philosophical line of enquiry and carries it further, saying that it is not just a matter of coming to an explanation of its own laws but that it has to do with an experience of thinking, an *experiential contemplation* of thinking by thinking itself. At this stage one must not only practise thinking about thinking—otherwise one would remain with Hegel or Aristotle, who also knew this—but also, even more importantly, carry out the exact observation of thinking as a real inner life process. This means, however, that the power must be found to unite individual thoughts and enable them to be strung together logically rather than arbitrarily, so that a regulated and harmonious thought organism develops in the soul.

This deeper power of thinking now needs to be consciously observed and understood. What is this power? It is the innermost power of thinking. One can also say: It is thinking itself. Through what can this power be observed? Also only through thinking itself. In this way, the exceptional state described in *The Philosophy of Spiritual Activity* comes about.[7] In it subject and object coincide for the first time in an inner experience.

Now one can ask: What is actually meant by abolishing and overcoming the opposition between, or the polarity of, subject and object? This is none other than consciously leaving the body. For as long as a person still remains completely inside his body, he always has in his consciousness this polarity of himself as subject and the world outside his body, which is only accessible to him through his sense perceptions and is therefore always an object for his experience; whereas if he can overcome this polarity in himself, he enters into the spiritual world with his thinking. He is then fully conscious outside his body and can consciously take hold of his real ego. This has to do with the human ego which from the outset lives and weaves outside the body, as is described in the Bologna lecture.

The thinking which can accomplish this is the third kind of thinking, which we can take into the spiritual world. It is at the same time the only guarantor of our ego presence outside the body in the spiritual world.

Rudolf Steiner had already mentioned this in his *Philosophy of Spiritual Activity*: 'Ego consciousness comes about through the physical organization. People should not confuse it with the contention that ego consciousness once created remains independent of the physical organization. Once created, it is taken up in thinking and continually shares *its spiritual essence*.'[8] This creates the firm foundation and the clear starting point for scientific research of the spiritual world which proceeds from the power of the human ego and is completely in accord with modern thinking.

★

If we now look back once more to Rudolf Steiner's youth from the foundation that has been arrived at, we find how he mastered these three kinds of thinking consistently and developed them further within himself. At the age of 14 he began to read philosophical books intensively. After graduating, he studied practically all sciences known at that time at the University of Vienna and with this grasped the first kind of thinking so to say from two sides—the philosophical and the scientific.

At the end of his student studies he was given the task of editing Goethe's scientific writings, with which he was occupied for 14 years (1883–1897) with unbelievable intensity. During this entire time he developed in himself the second, morphological type of thinking.

Then came the third stage—spiritual thinking. With this, Rudolf Steiner sought direct access to the higher human ego in the spiritual world. In this regard, he wrote a moving document as a 19-year-old indicating how he first personally experienced the higher ego after reading a passage in the philosopher Schelling's work. For Schelling it was a matter of beholding the spiritual capacity in man, the eternal in the self or ego, by immersing oneself in one's own being through stripping away all sense impressions. In other words, this had to do with experiencing man's eternal or, in the terminology of the Bologna lecture, transcendental ego.

The young Rudolf Steiner reported about this in a letter to a friend and ended the description with the following words: 'I believed and still think I have discovered this innermost ability quite clearly in myself—I have suspected it for a long time ... What is a sleepless night compared to such a discovery?'[9]

What was the actual consequence of this for Rudolf Steiner? Later, towards the end of his life, as he looked back at this period of his youth and at the reality of his experience at that time, he wrote in his autobiography about the significance that the human ego had for him then: 'To me this "ego" was an inwardly observable experience of a *reality* present in the experience. This reality appeared to me no less certain than anything recognized by materialism. But there is absolutely nothing material in it. For me this insight into the reality and spirituality of the "ego" in the following years has helped me rise above all materialistic temptations. I had come to know that the "ego" is unshakeable.'[10]

That didn't mean he had already reached his goal; for in order to find and comprehend the ego outside the body in the spiritual world consciously in its entirety, one must go through a further experience. This is not described in the Bologna lecture, probably because it was a public talk and the time Rudolf Steiner had available for his presentation was quite limited. This is the theme of the threshold to the spiritual world and its Guardian, which is a focal point on the anthroposophical path of schooling.[11] In a condition of profound self-knowledge one has to encounter oneself in the form of the Guardian at the threshold and experience oneself as one is perceived by the spiritual world, that is to say, as one really is without any self-deception, for this is now no longer possible. Above all, in meeting the Guardian a person must leave behind everything that connects him with the physical world. Nothing that binds a person to his body and sense experiences can be taken over the threshold. Only one thing may pass over the threshold, Rudolf Steiner says—that is the deepest power of thinking referred to above.

This is the modern path leading to the real human ego, which can only be found in the spiritual world on the other side of the threshold. In this regard, Rudolf Steiner says: 'This meeting [with the Guardian of the Threshold], does indeed take place, and has the effect of suddenly revealing to a person what he has become as an earthly human being in sensory existence. At the same time, it is self-knowledge in the truest, most comprehensive sense of the word. A person sees himself as he is; and he also sees himself as he ought to become! But people are not always able to see themselves in this way. Today I have only spoken about the world of concepts and ideas which must be discarded [at the threshold]. Much more must also be laid aside. When one reaches the Guardian of the Threshold, one must actually leave behind everything that one knows about oneself; but one must still retain *something* that can be taken over. That is what matters!'[12]

What is this mysterious 'something', which can be taken from the earth across the threshold into the spiritual world and can also exist purely and simply on the other side of the threshold? It is nothing other than the thinking of the third kind penetrated with full clarity and circumspection. Rudolf Steiner speaks about this in another context: 'The *only thing which should remain* to us is a thinking that is infused with will and circumspection. This thinking, however, now appears in a new form [meaning the third kind of thinking].... One is therefore plunging into a completely new world. Then one is in the higher worlds, where the ordinary world of the senses is left behind one as a memory.'[13]

Now one is on the other side of the threshold, where one is 'surrounded ... by beings, soul-spiritual beings, just as we are surrounded by sense-perceptible beings in the time between birth and death' (ibid.). Among these spiritual beings, it is possible to have a quite definite experience of the transcendental ego. For here a real supersensible being is among other equally real and independent beings in the spiritual world. We have now reached the main thrust of the Bologna lecture.

★

As we have already seen, the next step in the Bologna lecture is at least indicated: the step to a further goal, which at the same time is the actual object of the entire path. It is no longer a matter of merely grasping the higher ego but of attaining the *true ego*. But how does one arrive at this still higher experience? The description of how Rudolf Steiner achieved this goal is, I think, one of the most moving and dramatic moments in his initiation.

For here it is a matter of making a leap over the cosmic abyss. Rudolf Steiner indicates that two things are necessary for this: a sheer, unlimited *trust in spiritual life* and *help from beyond the world abyss*, which alone make this leap possible. The meeting with the true ego can take place only after successfully completing the entire path.

In reading the following, moving words of Rudolf Steiner, one should not forget that his own actual, inner experience lies behind them. It is the simple report about his initiation on the path to the true ego. The main question proceeding from this description is: who is the spiritual being coming from beyond the world abyss who makes it possible for a person to connect with his true ego, thus bringing to the person who dares to take this leap the true ego as the highest goal of his development? Even though Rudolf Steiner doesn't name this being, we discover immediately that this being can be identified from a broad knowledge of anthroposophy.

Let us now read Rudolf Steiner's words: 'It is something quite unusual to commit with full consciousness one's memory ego to obliteration, to forgetting, to the abyss, really to stand awhile in the spiritual world at the abyss of existence facing the great emptiness as nothingness. It is the most harrowing experience that a person can have and one must approach this state with great trust. In order to approach the abyss as nothing, it is necessary that one trusts that the true ego will be brought to one out of the [spiritual] world. This is what happens.... The ascent to the super-spiritual world is an inner experience,[14] the experience of a totally new world at the abyss of existence and the receiving of the true ego from this super-spiritual world.'[15]

We have already seen that from the outset the higher human ego lives and weaves in the spiritual world. However, we can take nothing from the Earth over the threshold into the spiritual world except real, enhanced thinking and the memory of our connection to the earthly world that we have left behind.

With the next step, this memory must also disappear, must consciously be extinguished by us. Nothing remains any more except the force of consciousness itself—the pure ego consciousness anchored in the innermost essence of thinking—as well as an infinite trust in the good forces of world existence, which must completely fill our soul in this moment. In former times one would have said that this is the power of faith. Now one calls it *trust*, because at the present time trust is rooted not in faith but in knowledge. Only on this condition can what is sought approach us from another shore. It is a gift to us. Now we have reached the stage of the inner path where the word *mercy* has its rightful place. Something of the nature of the most sublime grace is extended to us by a certain being of the super-spiritual world.

Here, if not before, one begins to suspect from whom this grace of man in the becoming, this bestowal of the true ego, can come. It comes from the world Ego, from Christ Himself. Man ascends to his true ego and in this manner experiences out of his own inner knowledge how the two streams referred to above now flow together. In searching for the essential nature of the human ego in the sense of the Bologna lecture—if one remains consistently devoted to this path and keeps advancing far enough along it—one meets Christ. In Him man now experiences the highest archetype of the human ego. One meets Him by comprehending the true ego in the profoundest depths of one's own being.

One then no longer experiences Christ outside oneself but within. He is then as clearly and unambiguously present in a person as is otherwise the case only with the third kind of thinking which has been spoken of here. In such a situation a person is wholly present in his full individuality. A union of *this* nature with Christ is only possible at the stage of Intuition.[16] That is the highest fulfilment of what Paul meant when he said: 'Not I, but the Christ in me' (Galatians 2:20).

In this there also lies the culmination of modern initiation, which leads to Christ and has its roots in thinking. For, as anthroposophy describes and represents it, the goal of this initiation is seeking and finding the true being of man. It leads from stage to stage into the spiritual world in order at the end of the path to understand the true human ego in full consciousness. Because, however, the true ego is inseparably connected with the Christ Being, the understanding of it leads at the same time to the new *Christ consciousness* within man. This is the consciousness which is so comprehensive that it can research both the supersensible and the sense-perceptible worlds; for Christ was and is the only God who descended from the higher worlds to the Earth and lived there as man among other human beings. He is, therefore, the only one in the spiritual world who possesses the consciousness that pervades everything in heaven and on Earth. He shares this new capacity with a person who on the path of modern initiation—whose most important characteristics are described in the Bologna lecture—has developed the Christ consciousness within himself out of his true ego. Hence this forms the actual source from which Rudolf Steiner could create his entire anthroposophy; for he himself had personal knowledge of the spiritual experiences of which we have briefly spoken here.[17]

Thus Rudolf Steiner gave birth within himself to anthroposophy as modern spiritual science out of a union with the true ego and, hence, out of a development of Christ consciousness. He could therefore know *from his own experience* what actually occurred on Earth nearly 2,000 years before at the Turning Point of Time—though in a wholly modern sense, that is, as a *celebration of knowledge.*

Many of you will recognize from his autobiography the moving words with which Rudolf Steiner describes the highest experience of his own initiation: 'My soul development rested on my having stood in spirit before the Mystery of Golgotha in a most inward, most solemn festival of knowledge.'[18]

★

We are now approaching the end of this lecture. We have seen where the path outlined in the Bologna lecture leads. We have also shown how closely this path was connected with Rudolf Steiner's own life and initiation; for he followed this path to its end in order that he might experience the essential nature of the Mystery of Golgotha in a festival of knowledge out of his connection with the true ego and found the whole of anthroposophy upon this central event of earthly evolution.

Hence anthroposophy is of a Christian nature not only because Rudolf Steiner spoke so much in his lectures and books about the Being of Christ and the central significance of the Mystery of Golgotha. No, anthroposophy is Christian because its method of research—how the spiritual world is researched through it—is Christian in the deepest sense. This is so because anthroposophical research springs solely from the new Christ consciousness and is only possible through it.

We find the roots of all this in the Bologna lecture. For there is a place in this lecture where the earthly ego and the true, higher human ego are contrasted. There it is said that the earthly ego—and with it also earthly ego consciousness—arises as a reflection of man's higher ego. This happens with the help of the physical body, which in this process assumes the role of a mirror in which the reflection of the ego appears, thus enabling a person to become conscious. The true (higher) ego however remains in the spiritual world and can only be found there. What lies in between? What is alone able to connect the two poles, these two egos, one of which one belongs to Earth and the other to heaven, with one another?

To answer this question, let us briefly consider our entire earthly civilization. On the one hand, there is its Western part, which is almost entirely oriented to the earthly ego. Western materialism continually makes the fundamental error of treating the mere image as if it were the being itself that is standing before the mirror.

In contrast, the nature of its Eastern counterpart is totally oriented to the higher ego. It really doesn't want to know anything about the Earth but seeks only to reach back to this higher ego, to the true ego which passes through different earthly lives. However, the East doesn't see any real sense in these repeated earthly lives and attaches no special significance to them, but would prefer to leave the eternal wheel of rebirths behind as quickly as possible.[19]

What is able to connect, to harmonize these polarities, these mighty one-sided contradictions with one another? In this regard, what makes the future of mankind on Earth inherently possible? Rudolf Steiner gives a clear indication of this in his Bologna lecture at the place where he talks about the third stage of supersensible knowledge, the stage of Intuition. He points out that both observation methods, one of which examines the physical world of the senses (the earthly ego) and the other the supersensible (the higher ego), must be 'supplemented by a [third] method coming to meet them, which enters into the depths of the problem and which is capable of beholding the synthesis of the sensible and the supersensible. The confluence of the two currents may be conceived as given through a possible further development of the life of the mind up to the intuitive cognition already described. Only within *this* is that polarity superseded.'[20]

We have seen that it is precisely at the stage of Intuition where the true human ego, which is so deeply connected with the Christ Being, can be grasped. There it is possible to unite both polarities in a synthesis, which at the same time is that of heaven and Earth and also represents the conscious path leading from Earth to heaven and back again.

The true ego
Synthesis

The earthly ego
Earthly knowledge

The higher ego
Spiritual knowledge

That we are able to follow this path to the end, as indicated in the Bologna lecture, we ultimately owe to the fact that almost 2000 years ago at the Turning Point of Time a divine Being descended from the spiritual worlds to the Earth and through the Mystery of Golgotha connected Himself for ever with mankind's development—the highest ego Being, who in reality exceeds all of our conceptions. It is that Being, who represents the model and archetype of every human ego for all future ages, who alone gives us the possibility to reach the ultimate goal on the path described.

All this stands behind the simple sentence where at the end of his life Rudolf Steiner referred to this future: ' "Christ gives me my humanity"—that will be the fundamental feeling which will well up in the soul and pervade it.'[21] By this is meant the human being who is able to embrace his true ego.

However, something else was also necessary in order to find the path depicted in the Bologna lecture; for the divine Being brings to free mankind today only the *possibility* of a new development. Every person must fulfill this possibility consciously and freely, otherwise his freedom is not guaranteed.

Therefore, it is essential that there are always such people who take hold of this possibility out of full freedom and make it a reality in their own lives in order to make it possible for mankind to achieve the goal of its entire development.

From all that has been presented here, one may conclude that the person who not only described to mankind the path to this goal but also inaugurated it and was the first one in our time to follow it to the end, thus revealing to all present-day people through his whole life and work what it signifies to achieve the true ego and an activity deriving from a consciousness of Christ—this man was *Rudolf Steiner.*

This is what I have attempted to show you this evening during the 150th anniversary of the birthday of this special person.

Part II

Rudolf Steiner

THE FOUNDATIONS OF ANTHROPOSOPHICAL METHODOLOGY

1. Lecture held in Bologna on 8 April 1911 at the Fourth International Philosophy Conference

The Psychological Foundations of Anthroposophy and its Standpoint in Relation to the Theory of Knowledge

The task which I should like to undertake in the following exposition is that of discussing the scientific character and value of a spiritual trend to which a widespread inclination would still deny the designation 'scientific.' This spiritual trend bears—in allusion to various endeavors of its kind in the present period—the name theosophy. In the history of philosophy, this name has been applied to certain spiritual trends which have emerged again and again in the course of the cultural life of humanity, with which, however, what is to be presented here does not at all coincide, although it bears many reminders of them. For this reason we shall limit our consideration here to what can be described in the course of our exposition as a special condition of the mind, and we shall disregard opinions which may be held in reference to much of what is customarily called theosophy. Only by adhering to this point of view will it be possible to give precise expression to the manner in which one may view the relationship between the spiritual trend we have in mind and the types of conception characterizing contemporary science and philosophy.

Let it be admitted without reservation that, even regarding the very concept of knowledge, it is difficult to establish a relationship between what is customarily called theosophy and everything that seems to be firmly established at present as constituting the idea of 'science' and 'knowledge', and which has brought and surely will continue to bring such great benefits to human culture. The last few centuries have led to the practice of recognizing as 'scientific' only what can be tested readily by anyone at any time through observation, experiment, and the elaboration of these by the human intellect. Everything that possesses significance only within the subjective experiences of the human mind must be excluded from the category of what is scientifically established. Now, it will scarcely be denied that the philosophical concept of knowledge has for a long time adjusted itself to the scientific type of conception just described. This can best be recognized from the investigations which have been carried out in our time as to what can constitute a possible object of human knowledge, and at what point this knowledge has to admit its limits. It would be superfluous for me to support this statement by an outline of contemporary inquiries in the field of the theory of knowledge. I should like to emphasize only the objective aimed at in those inquiries. In connection with them, it is presupposed that the relationship of man to the external world affords a determinable concept of the nature of the process of cognition, and that this concept of knowledge provides a basis for characterizing what lies within the reach of cognition. However greatly the trends in theories of knowledge may diverge from one another, if the above characterization is taken in a sufficiently broad sense, there will be found within it that which characterizes a common element in the decisive philosophical trends.

Now, the concept of knowledge belonging to what is here called anthroposophy is such that it apparently contradicts the concept just described. It conceives knowledge to be something the character of which cannot be deduced directly from the observation of the nature of the human being and his relationship to the external world. On the basis of established facts of the life of the mind, anthroposophy believes itself justified in asserting that knowledge is not something finished, complete in itself, but something fluid, capable of evolution. It believes itself justified in pointing out that, beyond the horizon of the normally conscious life of the mind, there is another into which the human being can penetrate. And it is necessary to emphasize that the life of the mind here referred to is not to be understood as that which is at present customarily designated as the 'subconscious'. This 'subconscious' may be the object of scientific research; from the point of view of the usual methods in research, it can be made an object of inquiry, as are other facts of the life of nature and of the mind. But this has nothing to do with that condition of the mind to which we are referring, within which the human being is as completely conscious, possesses as complete logical watchfulness over himself, as within the limits of the ordinary consciousness. But this condition of the mind must first be created by means of certain exercises, certain experiences of the soul. It cannot be presupposed as a given fact in the nature of man. This condition of mind represents something which may be designated as a further development of the life of the human mind without the cessation, during the course of this further development, of self-possession and other evidences of the mind's conscious life.

I wish to characterize this condition of mind and then to show how what is acquired through it may be included under the scientific concepts of knowledge belonging to our age. My present task shall be, therefore, to describe the method employed within this spiritual trend on the basis of a possible development of the mind. This first part of my exposition may be called:

A Spiritual–Scientific Mode of Perception Based upon Potential Psychological Facts

What is here described is to be regarded as experiences of the mind of which one may become aware if certain prerequisite conditions are first brought about in the mind. The epistemological value of these experiences shall be tested only after they have first been simply described.

What is to be undertaken may be designated as a 'mental exercise'. The initial step consists in considering from a different point of view contents of the mind which are ordinarily evaluated to their worth as copies of an external item of reality. In the concepts and ideas which the human being forms he wishes to have at first what may be a copy, or at least a token, of something existing outside of the concepts or ideas. The spiritual researcher, in the sense here intended, seeks for mental contents which are similar to the concept and ideas of ordinary life or of scientific research; but he does not consider their cognitional value in relation to an objective entity, but lets them exist in his mind as operative forces. He plants them as spiritual seed, so to speak, in the soil of the mind's life, and awaits in complete serenity of spirit their effect upon this life of the mind. He can then observe that, with the repeated employment of such an exercise, the condition of the mind undergoes a change. It must be expressly emphasized, however, that what really counts is the repetition. For the fact in question is not that the content of the concepts in the ordinary sense brings something about in the mind after the manner of a process of cognition; on the contrary, we have to do with an actual process in the life of the mind itself. In this process, concepts do not play the role of cognitional elements but that of real forces; and their effect depends upon having the same forces lay hold in frequent repetition upon the mind's life. The effect achieved in the mind depends pre-eminently upon the requirement that the same force shall again and again seize upon the experience connected with the concept. For this reason the greatest results can be attained through meditations upon the same content which are repeated at definite intervals through relatively long periods of time. The duration of such a meditation is, in this connection, of little importance. It may be very brief, provided only that it is accompanied by absolute serenity of soul and the complete exclusion from the mind of all external sense impressions and all ordinary activity of the intellect. What is essential is the seclusion of the mind's life with the content indicated. This must be mentioned because it needs to be clearly understood that undertaking these exercises of the mind need not disturb anyone in his ordinary life. The time required is available, as a rule, to everyone. And, if the exercises are rightly carried out, the change which they bring about in the mind does not produce the slightest effect upon the constitution of consciousness necessary for the normal human life. (The fact that—because of what the human being actually is in his present status—undesirable excesses and peculiarities sometimes occur cannot alter in any way one's judgement of the essential nature of the practice.)

For the discipline of the mind which has been described, most concepts in human life are scarcely at all usable. All contents of the mind which relate in marked degree to objective elements outside of themselves have little effect if used for the exercises we have characterized. In far greater measure are mental pictures suitable which can be designated as emblems, as symbols.

Most fruitful of all are those which relate in a living way comprehensively to a manifold content. Let us take as an example, proven by experience to be good, what Goethe designated as his idea of the 'archetypal plant'. It may be permissible to refer to the fact that, during a conversation with Schiller, he once drew with a few strokes a symbolic picture of this 'archetypal plant'. Moreover, he said that one who makes this picture alive in his mind possesses in it something out of which it would be possible to devise, through modification in conformity with law, all possible forms capable of existence. Whatever one may think about the objective cognitional value of such a 'symbolic archetypal plant', if it is made to live in the mind in the manner indicated, if one awaits in serenity its effects upon the mind's life, there comes about something which can be called a changed constitution of mind.

The mental pictures which are said by spiritual scientists to be usable in this connection may at times seem decidedly strange. This feeling of strangeness can be eliminated if one reflects that such representations must not be considered for their value as truths in the ordinary sense, but should be viewed with respect to the manner in which they are effective as real forces in the mind's life. The spiritual scientist does not attribute value to the significance of the pictures which are used for the mental exercises, but to what is experienced in the mind under their influence.

Here we can give, naturally, only a few examples of effective symbolic representations. Let one conceive the being of man in a mental image in such a way that the lower human nature, related to the animal organization, shall appear in its relation to man as a spiritual being, through the symbolic union of an animal shape and the most highly idealized human form superimposed upon this—somewhat, let us say, like a centaur. The more pictorially alive the symbol appears, the more saturated with content, the better it is. Under the conditions described, this symbol acts in such a way on the mind that, after the passage of a certain time—of course, somewhat long—the inner life processes are felt to be strengthened in themselves, mobile, reciprocally illuminating one another. An old symbol which may be used with good result is the so-called staff of Mercury—that is, the mental image of a straight line around which a spiral curves. Of course, one must picture this figure as emblematic of a force-system—in such a way, let us say, that along the straight line there runs one force system, to which there corresponds another of lower velocity passing through the spiral. (Concretely expressed, one may conceive in connection with this figure the growth of the stem of a plant and the corresponding sprouting of leaves along its length. Or one may take it as an image of an electro-magnet. Still further, there can emerge in this way a picture of the development of a human being, the enhancing capacities being symbolized by the straight line, the manifold impressions corresponding with the course of the spiral.)

Mathematical forms may become especially significant, to the extent that symbols of cosmic processes can be seen in them. A good example is the so-called 'Cassini curve', with its three figures—the form resembling an ellipse, the lemniscate, and that which consists of two corresponding branches. In such a case the important thing is to experience the mental image in such a way that certain appropriate impressions in the mind shall accompany the transition of one curve form into the other in accordance with mathematical principles.

Other exercises may then be added to these. They consist also in symbols, but such as correspond with representations which may be expressed in words. Let one think, through the symbol of light, of the wisdom which may be pictured as living and weaving in the orderly processes of the cosmic phenomena. Wisdom which expresses itself in sacrificial love may be thought of as symbolized by warmth which comes about in the presence of light. One may think of sentences—which, therefore, have only a symbolic character—fashioned out of such concepts. The mind can be absorbed in meditating upon such sentences. The result depends essentially upon the degree of serenity and seclusion of soul within the symbol to which one attains in the meditation. If success is achieved, it consists in the fact that the soul feels as if lifted out of the corporeal organization. It experiences something like a change in its sense of existence. If we agree that, in normal life, the feeling of the human being is such that his conscious life, proceeding from a unity, takes on a specific character in harmony with the representations which are derived from the percepts brought by the individual senses, then the result of the exercises is that the mind feels itself permeated by an experience of itself not so sharply differentiated in transition from one part of the experience to another as, for example, colour and tone representations are differentiated within the horizon of the ordinary consciousness. The mind has the experience that it can withdraw into a region of inner being which it owes to the success of the exercises and which was something empty, something which could not be perceived, before the exercises were undertaken.

Before such an inner experience is reached, there occur many transitional stages in the condition of the mind. One of these manifests itself in an attentive observation—to be acquired through the exercise—of the moment of awaking out of sleep. It is possible then to feel clearly how, out of something not hitherto known to one, forces lay hold systematically upon the structure of the bodily organization. One feels, as if in a remembered concept, an after-effect of influences from this something, which have been at work upon the corporeal organization during sleep. And if the person has acquired, in addition, the capacity to experience within his corporeal organization the something here described, he will perceive clearly the difference between the relationship of this something to the body in the waking and in the sleeping state. He cannot then do otherwise than to say that during the waking state this something is inside the body and during the sleeping state it is outside. One must not, however, associate ordinary spatial conception with this 'inside' and 'outside', but must use these terms only to designate the specific experiences of a mind which has carried out the exercises described.

These exercises are of an intimate soul-character. They take for each person an individual form. When the beginning is once made, the individual element results from a particular use of the soul to be brought about in the course of the exercises. But what follows with utter necessity is the positive consciousness of living within a reality independent of the external corporeal organization and supersensible in character. For the sake of simplicity, let us call such a person seeking for the described soul experiences a 'spiritual researcher' [*Geistesforscher*]. For such a spiritual researcher, there exists the definite consciousness—kept under complete self-possession—that, behind the bodily organization perceptible to the senses, there is a supersensible organization, and that it is possible to experience oneself within this as the normal consciousness experiences itself within the physical bodily organization. (The exercises referred to can be indicated here only in principle. A detailed presentation may be found in my book, *Knowledge of the Higher Worlds and Its Attainment.*)

Through appropriate continuation of the exercises, the 'something' we have described passes over into a sort of spiritually organized condition. The consciousness becomes clearly aware that it is in relationship with a supersensible world in a cognitional way, in a manner similar to that in which it is related through the senses to the sense world. It is quite natural that serious doubt at once arises, regarding the assertion of such a cognitional relationship of the supersensible part of the being of man to the surrounding world. There may be an inclination to relegate everything which is thus experienced to the realm of illusion, hallucination, auto-suggestion, and the like. A theoretical refutation of such doubt is, from the very nature of things, impossible. For the question here cannot be that of a theoretical exposition regarding the existence of a supersensible world, but only that of possible experiences and observations which are presented to the consciousness in precisely the same way in which observations are mediated through the external sense organs. For the corresponding supersensible world, therefore, no other sort of recognition can be demanded than that which the human being offers to the world of colours, tones, etc. Yet consideration must be given to the fact that, when the exercises are carried out in the right way—and, most important, with never relaxed self-possession—the spiritual researcher can discern through immediate experience the difference between the imagined supersensible and that which is actually experienced; just as certainly as in the sense world one can discern the difference between imagining the feel of a piece of hot iron and actually touching it. Precisely concerning the differences among hallucination, illusion, and supersensible reality, the spiritual researcher acquires through his exercises a practice more and more unerring. But it is also natural that the prudent spiritual researcher must be extremely critical regarding individual supersensible observations made by him. He will never speak otherwise about positive findings of supersensible research than with the reservation that one thing or another has been observed and that the critical caution practised in connection with this justifies the assumption that anyone will make the same observations who, by means of the appropriate exercises, can establish a relationship with the supersensible world. Differences among the pronouncements of individual spiritual researchers cannot really be viewed in any other light than the different pronouncements of various travellers who have visited the same region and who describe it.

In my book, *Knowledge of the Higher Worlds and Its Attainment,* that world which, in the manner described, appears above the horizon of consciousness has been called—in accordance with the practice of those who have been occupied as spiritual researchers in the same field—'the imaginative world'. But one must dissociate from this expression, used in a purely technical sense, anything suggesting a world created by mere 'fancy'. Imaginative is intended merely to suggest the qualitative character of the content of the mind. This mental content resembles in its form the 'imaginations' of ordinary consciousness, except that an imagination in the physical world is not directly related to something real, whereas the imaginations of the spiritual researcher are just as unmistakably to be ascribed to a supersensibly real entity as the mental picture of a colour in the sense world, for instance, is ascribed to an objectively real entity.

But the 'imaginative world' and the knowledge of it mark only the first step for the spiritual researcher, and very little more is to be learned through it about the supersensible world than its external side. A further step is required. This consists in a further deepening of the life of the soul than that which has been considered in connection with the first step. Through intense concentration upon the soul life, brought about by the exercises, the spiritual researcher must render himself capable of completely eliminating the content of the symbols from his consciousness. What he then still has to hold firmly within his consciousness is only the process to which his inner life was subjected while he was absorbed in the symbols. The content of the symbols pictured must be cast out in a sort of real abstraction and only the form of the experience in connection with the symbols must remain in the consciousness. The unreal symbolic character of the forming of mental images—which was significant only for a transitional stage of the soul's development—is thereby eliminated, and the consciousness uses as the object of its meditation the inner weaving of the mind's content. What can be described of such a process actually compares with the real experience of the mind as a feeble shadow compares with the object which casts the shadow. What appears simple in the description derives its very significant effect from the psychic energy which is exerted.

The living and moving within the content of the soul, thus rendered possible, can be called a real beholding of oneself. The inner being of man thus learns to know itself not merely through reflecting about itself as the bearer of the sense impressions and the elaborator of these sense impressions through thinking; on the contrary, it learns to know itself as it is, without relationship to a content coming from the senses; it experiences itself in itself, as supersensible reality. This experience is not like that of the ego when in ordinary self-observation, attention is withdrawn from the things cognized in the environment and is directed back to the cognizing self. In this case, the content of consciousness shrinks more and more down to the point of the 'ego'. Such is not the case in the real beholding of the self by the spiritual researcher. In this, the soul content becomes continuously richer in the course of the exercises. It consists in one's living within law-conforming interrelationships; and the self does not feel, as in the case of the laws of nature, which are abstracted from the phenomena of the external world, that it is outside the web of laws; but, on the contrary, it is aware of itself as within this web; it experiences itself as one with these laws.

The danger which may come about at this stage of the exercises lies in the fact that the person concerned may believe too early—because of deficiency in true self-possession—that he has arrived at the right result, and may then feel the mere after-effects of the symbolic inner pictures to be an inner life. Such an inner life is obviously valueless, and must not be mistaken for the inner life which appears at the right moment, making itself known to true circumspection through the fact that, although it manifests complete reality, yet it resembles no reality hitherto known.

To an inner life thus attained, there is now the possibility of a supersensible knowledge characterized by a higher degree of certitude than that of mere imaginative cognition. At this point in the soul's development, the following manifestation occurs. The inner experience gradually becomes filled with a content which enters the mind from without in a manner similar to that in which the content of sense perception enters through the senses from the outer world. Only, the filling of the mind with the supersensible content consists in an actual living within this content. If one wishes to employ a comparison with a fact taken from ordinary life, it may be said that the entering of the ego into union with a spiritual content is now experienced as one experiences the entering of the ego into union with a mental picture retained in memory. Yet there is the distinction that the content of that with which one enters into union cannot be compared in any respect with something previously experienced and that it cannot be related to something past but only to something present. Knowledge of this character may well be called knowledge 'through inspiration', provided nothing except what has been described is associated in thought with this term. I have used the expression thus as a technical term in my book, *Knowledge of the Higher Worlds and Its Attainment.*

In connection with this 'knowledge through inspiration', a new experience now appears. That is, the manner in which one becomes aware of the content of the mind is entirely subjective. At first, this content does not manifest itself as objective. One knows it as something experienced; but one does not feel that one confronts it. This comes about only after one has through soul-energy condensed it, in a sense, within itself. Only thus does it become something which can be looked at objectively. But, in this process of the psyche, one becomes aware that, between the physical bodily organization and that something which has been separated from this by the exercises, there is still another entity. If one desires names for these things, one may employ those which have become customary in so-called theosophy—provided one does not connect with these names all sorts of fantastic associations, but designates by them solely what has been described. That 'something' in which the self lives as in an entity free from the bodily organization is called the astral body; and that which is discovered between this astral body and the physical organism is called the etheric body. (One is, of course, not to connect this in thought with the 'ether' of modern physics.)

Now, it is from the etheric body that the forces come, through which the self is enabled to make an objective perception of the subjective content of inspired knowledge. By what right, it may be asked with good reason, does the spiritual researcher come to the standpoint of ascribing this perception to a supersensible world instead of considering it a mere creation of his own self? He would have no right to do this if the etheric body, which he experiences in connection with his psychic process, did not in its inner conformity to law compel him to do so with objective necessity. But such is the case, for the etheric body is experienced as a confluence of the all-encompassing complex of laws of the macrocosm. The important point is not how much of this complex of laws becomes the actual content of the spiritual researcher's consciousness. The peculiar fact is that direct cognition sees clearly that the etheric body is nothing else than a compacted image reflecting in itself the cosmic web of laws. Knowledge of the etheric body by the spiritual researcher does not at first extend to showing what content from the sum total of the universal cosmic web of laws is reflected by this formation, but to showing what this content is.

Other justifiable doubts which the ordinary consciousness must raise against spiritual research, together with much besides, are the following. One may take note of the findings of this research (as they appear in contemporary literature) and may say: 'Actually, what you there describe as the content of supersensible knowledge proves upon closer scrutiny to be nothing more, after all, than combinations of ordinary conceptions taken from the sense world.' And, in fact, this is what is said. (Likewise, the descriptions of the higher worlds which I myself felt justified in giving in the volumes, *Theosophy* and *Occult Science, an Outline,* are found to be, so it seems, nothing but combinations of conceptions taken from the sense world—as, for instance, when the evolution of the earth through combinations of entities of warmth, light, etc., is described.)

Against this view, however, the following must be said. When the spiritual researcher wishes to give expression to his experiences, he is compelled to employ the means available to sense-conceptions for expressing what is experienced in a supersensible sphere. His experience is not to be conceived, then, as if it were like his means of expression, but with the realization that he uses this means only like the words of a language which he requires. One must seek for the content of his experience, not in the means of expression—that is, not in the illustrative representations—but in the manner in which he uses these instruments of expression. The difference between his presentation and a fantastic combining of sensible representations lies in the fact that fantastic combining arises out of a subjective arbitrariness, whereas the presentation of the spiritual researcher rests upon a conscious familiarity with the supersensible complex of laws, acquired through practice. Here, however, the reason is also to be found why the presentations of the spiritual researcher may so easily be misunderstood. That is, the manner in which he speaks is more important than what he says. In the *how* is reflected his supersensible experience. If the objection is raised that, in this case, what the spiritual researcher says has no direct relationship with the ordinary world, it must be emphasized in reply that the manner of his presentation does, in fact, meet the practical requirements for an explanation of the sense world drawn from a supersensible sphere, and that the understanding of the world process perceptible to the senses is aided by real attention to the findings of the spiritual researcher.

Another objection may be raised. It may be asked what the assertions of the spiritual researcher have to do with the content of ordinary consciousness, since this consciousness, it may be said, cannot subject them to testing. Precisely this latter statement is, in principle, untrue. For research in the supersensible world, for discovering its facts, that condition of mind is necessary which can be acquired only by means of the exercises described. But this does not apply to the testing. For this purpose, when the spiritual researcher has communicated his findings, ordinary unprejudiced logic is sufficient. This will always be able to determine in principle that, if what the spiritual researcher says is true, the course of the world and of life as they proceed before the senses becomes understandable. The opinion which may be formed at first concerning the experiences of the spiritual researcher is not the important point. These may be viewed as hypotheses, regulative principles (in the sense of Kantian philosophy). But if they are simply applied to the sense world, it will be seen that the sense world confirms in the course of its events everything which is asserted by the spiritual researcher. (Naturally, this is valid only in principle; it is obvious that, in details, the assertions of so-called spiritual researchers may contain the gravest errors.)

Another experience of the spiritual researcher can come about only provided the exercises are carried still further. This continuation must consist in the fact that the spiritual researcher, after having attained to beholding the self, shall be able by energetic power of will to suppress this experience. He must be able to free the mind from everything that has been achieved through the continued after-effects of his exercises resting upon the outer sense world. The symbol-images are combined out of sense-images. The living and moving of the self within itself in connection with achieved inspired knowledge is, to be sure, free from the content of the symbols, yet it is a result of the exercises which have been carried out under their influence. Even though the inspired knowledge thus brings about a direct relationship of the self to the supersensible world, the clear beholding of the relationship can be carried still further. This results from the energetic suppression of the self-view which has been attained. After this suppression, the self may, as one possibility, be confronted by a void. In this case the exercises must be continued. As a second possibility, the self may find that it is more immediately in the presence of the supersensible world in its real being than it had been in connection with inspired knowledge. In the latter experience, there appears only the relationship of a supersensible world to the self; in the case of the kind of knowledge we are now describing the self is completely eliminated. If one wishes an expression adapted to ordinary consciousness for this condition of mind, it may be said that consciousness now experiences itself as the stage upon which a supersensible content, consisting of real being, is not merely perceived but perceives itself. (In the volume, *Knowledge of the Higher Worlds and Its Attainment*, I have called this kind of knowledge 'intuitive knowledge', but in connection with this expression the ordinary term intuition must be disregarded—which is used to designate every direct experience of a content of consciousness through feeling.)

Through intuitive knowledge, the whole relationship in which the human being as 'soul' finds himself with respect to his bodily organization is altered for the direct observation of the inner being of the soul. Before the faculty of spiritual vision, the etheric body appears, in a sense, as a supersensible organism differentiated within itself. And one recognizes its differentiated members as adapted in a definite way to the members of the physical bodily organization. The etheric body is experienced as the primary entity and the physical body as its copy, as something secondary. The horizon of consciousness appears to be determined through the law-conforming activity of the etheric body. The coordination of the phenomena within this horizon results from the activity of the differentiated members of the etheric body striving towards a unity. The etheric body rests upon an all-embracing cosmic web of laws; basic in the unification of its action is the tendency to relate itself to something as a centre. And the image of this uniting tendency is the physical body. Thus the latter proves to be an expression of the World-Ego, as the etheric body is an expression of the macrocosmic web of laws.

What is here set forth becomes clearer if we refer to a special fact of the inner life of the soul. This shall be done with reference to memory. As a result of the freeing of the self from the bodily organization, the spiritual researcher experiences the act of recollecting differently from one with ordinary consciousness. For him, recollecting, which is otherwise a more-or-less undifferentiated process, is separated into partial factors. At first, he senses the attraction toward an experience which is to be remembered, like a drawing of the attention in a certain direction. The experience is thus really analogous to the spatial directing of one's look toward a distant object, which one has first seen, then turns away from, and then turns toward again. The essential aspect of this is that the experience pressing toward remembrance is sensed as something which has stopped far away within the temporal horizon, and which does not merely have to be drawn up from the depths below in the soul's life. This turning in the direction of the experience pressing toward remembrance is at first a merely subjective process. When the remembrance now actually occurs, the spiritual researcher feels that it is the resistance of the physical body which works like a reflecting surface and raises the experience into the objective world of representations. Thus the spiritual researcher feels, in connection with the process of remembering, an occurrence which (subjectively perceptible) takes place within the etheric body and which becomes his remembrance through its reflection by the physical body. The first factor in recollecting would give merely disconnected experiences of the self. Through the fact that every remembrance is reflected by being impressed upon the life of the physical body, it becomes a part of the ego-experiences.

From all that has been said it is clear that the spiritual researcher comes to the point in his inner experience where he recognizes that the human being perceptible to the senses is the manifestation of a human being who is supersensible. He seeks for a consciousness of this supersensible human being, not by way of inference and speculation based upon the world that is directly given, but, on the contrary, by so transforming his own condition of mind that this ascends from the perceiving of the sense-perceptible to real participation in the supersensible. He arrives in this way at the recognition of a content of soul which proves to be richer, more filled with substance, than that of ordinary consciousness. What this road then leads to further can only be suggested here, of course, since a thorough exposition would require a comprehensive treatise. The inner being of the soul becomes for the spiritual researcher the producer, the builder, of that which constitutes the single human life in the physical world. And this producer manifests in itself that it has—interwoven into its life as realities—the forces, not only of the one life, but of many lives. That which may be considered as evidence of reincarnation, of repeated earthly lives, becomes a matter of actual observation. For what one learns of the inner core of the human life reveals, one might say, the telescoping together of interrelated human personalities. And these personalities can be sensed only in the relationship of the preceding and the succeeding. For one which follows is always manifested as the result of another. There is, moreover, in the relationship of one personality to another no element of continuity; rather, there is such a relationship as manifests itself in successive earthly lives separated by intervening periods of purely spiritual existence. To the observation of the soul's inner being, the periods during which the core of the human being was embodied in a physical corporeal organization are differentiated from those of the supersensible existence through the fact that, in the former, the experience of the content of the mind appears as if projected against the background of the physical life; while, in the latter, it appears as merged in a supersensible element which extends into the indefinite. It has not been the intention to present here anything more concerning so-called reincarnation than a sort of view of a perspective which is opened by the preceding reflections.

Anyone who admits the possibility that the human self may be able to become familiar with the core of being which is supersensibly visible will also no longer consider it unreasonable to suppose that, after further insight into this core of being, its content is revealed as differentiated, and that this differentiation provides the spiritual view of a succession of forms of existence extending back into the past. The fact that these forms of existence may bear their own time-indications may be seen to be intelligible through the analogy with ordinary memory. An experience appearing in memory bears in its content also its own time-indication. But the real 'resurvey in memory' of past forms of existence, supported by rigid self-supervision, is still very remote, of course, from the training of the spiritual researcher which has thus far been described, and great difficulties for the inner soul life tower up on the path before this can be attained in an incontestable form. Nevertheless, this lies on the direct continuation of the path to knowledge which has been described. It has been my desire at first to register here, so to speak, facts of experience in the inner soul-observation. It is for this reason that I have described reincarnation only as one such fact, but this fact can be established also on a theoretical basis. This I have done in the chapter entitled 'Karma and Reincarnation' in the book, *Theosophy*. I undertook there to show that certain findings of modem natural science, if thought out to their conclusion, lead to the assumption of the ideas of reincarnation of the human being.

Regarding the total nature of the human being, we must conclude from what has been said that his essential nature becomes understandable when viewed as the result of the interaction of the four members: 1) the physical bodily organization; 2) the etheric body; 3) the astral body; 4) the ego (the 'I'), which develops in the last-named member and comes to manifestation through the relationship between the central core of man's being and the physical organization. It is not possible to deal with the further articulation of these four life-manifestations of the total human being within the limits of one lecture. Here the intention has been to show only the basis of spiritual research. Further details I have sought to provide: 1) as to the method, in the volume, *Knowledge of the Higher Worlds and its Attainment;* and, 2) as to the system, in *Theosophy* and *Occult Science, an Outline.*

The Experiences of the Spiritual Researcher and the Theory of Knowledge

The exposition which has been presented will render it clear that anthroposophy, rightly understood, rests upon the foundation of a way of developing the human soul which is to be rigidly systematized in its character, and that it would be erroneous to suppose that there exists in the condition of mind of the spiritual researcher anything of the nature of what is ordinarily called at present enthusiasm, ecstasy, rapture, vision, and the like. Misunderstandings arise which may be presented in opposition to anthroposophy precisely through the confusion between the condition of mind here characterized and these other conditions. First, the belief is created through this confusion that there exists in the mind of the spiritual researcher a state of rapture, of being transported beyond self-possession in one's consciousness, a sort of striving after immediate instinctive vision. But the truth is just the opposite. The condition of mind of the spiritual researcher is even further removed than is ordinary consciousness from what is ordinarily called ecstasy, vision, from every sort of ordinary seership. Even such states of mind as those to which Shaftesbury refers are nebulous inner worlds in comparison with what is striven for by means of the exercises of the genuine spiritual researcher. Shaftesbury finds that by means of the 'cold intellect', without the rapture of the feeling nature, no path can be discovered leading to deeper forms of knowledge. True spiritual research carries with it the whole inner mental apparatus of logic and self-conscious circumspection when it seeks to transfer consciousness from the sensible to the supersensible sphere. It cannot be accused, therefore, of disregarding the rational element of knowledge. It can, however, elaborate its contents in concepts through thinking after perception, for the reason that, in passing out of the sense world, it always carries with it the rational element and always retains it, like a skeleton of the supersensible experience, as an integrating factor of all supersensible perception.

Naturally, it is impossible here to show the relationship of spiritual research to the various contemporary trends in theories of knowledge. The effort will be made by means of a few rather sketchy observations, therefore, to point out that particular conception of the theory of knowledge and its relationship to spiritual research which must experience the greatest difficulties in relation to spiritual research. It is, perhaps, not immodest to call attention to the fact that a complete basis for discrimination between philosophy and anthroposophy can be obtained from my two publications, *Truth and Science* and *The Philosophy of Freedom*.

To the epistemology of our time it has become increasingly axiomatic to maintain that there are given in the content of our consciousness only pictures, or even only 'tokens' (Helmholtz) of the transcendent–real. It will be needless to explain here how critical philosophy and physiology ('specific sense-energies', views of Johannes Müller and his adherents) have worked together to make of such a conception an apparently irrefutable idea. Naive Realism, which views the phenomena within the horizon of consciousness as something more than subjective representations of something objective, was considered in the philosophical development of the nineteenth century to have been invalidated for all time. But from that which lies at the foundation of this conception, there follows almost as a matter of course the rejection of the anthroposophical point of view. From the critical point of view, the anthroposophical viewpoint can be considered only as an impossible leap over the limits of knowledge inherent in the nature of our consciousness. If we may reduce to a simple formula an immeasurably great and brilliant expression of the critical theory of knowledge, it may be said that the critical philosopher sees in the facts within the horizon of consciousness representations, pictures, or tokens, and holds that a possible relationship to a transcendental external can be found only within the thinking consciousness. He holds that consciousness, of course, cannot leap beyond itself, cannot get outside itself, in order to plunge into a transcendental entity. Such a conception, in fact, has within it something that seems self-evident, and yet it rests upon a presupposition which one need only see into in order to refute it. It seems almost paradoxical when one brings against the subjective idealism expressed in the conception just cited the charge of a veiled materialism. And yet one cannot do otherwise. Permit me to render clear by a comparison what can be said here. Let a name be impressed in wax with a seal. The name, with everything pertaining to it, has been transferred by the seal into the wax. What cannot pass across from the seal into the wax is the metal of the seal. For the wax, substitute the soul life of the human being and for the seal substitute the transcendental. It then becomes obvious at once that one cannot declare it impossible for the transcendental to pass over into the impression unless one conceives the objective content of the transcendental as not spiritual, since this passing over of a spiritual content could be conceived in analogy with the complete reception of the name into the wax. To serve the requirement of Critical Idealism, the assumption would have to be made that the content of the transcendental is to be conceived in analogy with the metal of the seal. But this cannot be done otherwise than by making the veiled materialistic assumption that the transcendental must be received into the impression in the form of a materially conceived flowing-across. In the event that the transcendental is spiritual, it is entirely possible that the impression could take this up.

A further displacement in the simple facts of consciousness is caused by Critical Idealism through the fact that it leaves out of account the question of the factual relationship existing between the cognitional content and the ego. If one assumes *a priori* that the ego, together with the content of laws of the world reduced to the form of ideas and concepts, is outside the transcendental, it will be simply self-evident that this ego cannot leap beyond itself—that is, that it must always remain outside the transcendental. But this presupposition cannot be sustained in the face of an unbiased observation of the facts of consciousness. For the sake of simplicity, we shall here refer to the content of the cosmic web of law in so far as this can be expressed in mathematical concepts and formulae. The inner conformity to law in the relationships of mathematical forms is acquired within consciousness and is then applied to empirical factual situations. Now, no distinction can be discovered between what exists in consciousness as a mathematical concept when, on the one hand, this consciousness relates its own content to an empirical factual situation, and when, on the other, it visualizes this mathematical concept within itself in pure abstract mathematical thinking. But this signifies nothing else than that the ego, with its mathematical representation, is not outside the transcendental mathematical law-conformity of things but inside this. Therefore, one will arrive at a better conception of the ego from the viewpoint of the theory of knowledge, not by conceiving the ego as inside the bodily organization and receiving impressions 'from without', but by conceiving the ego as being itself within the law-conformity of things, and viewing the bodily organization as only a sort of mirror which reflects back to the ego through the organic bodily activity the living and moving of the ego outside the body in the transcendental. If, as regards mathematical thinking, one has familiarized oneself with the thought that the ego is not in the body but outside it, and that the bodily activity represents only the living mirror, from which the life of the ego in the transcendental is reflected, one can then find this thought epistemologically comprehensible concerning everything which appears within the horizon of consciousness.

One could then no longer say that the ego would have to leap beyond itself if it desired to enter the transcendental; but one would have to see that the ordinary empirical content of consciousness is related to that which is truly experienced in the inner life of man's core of being as the mirrored image is related to the real being of the person who is viewing himself in the mirror.

Through such a manner of conceiving in relation to the theory of knowledge, conflict could be decisively eliminated between natural science, with its inclination toward materialism, and a spiritual research, which presupposes the spiritual. For a right of way should be established for natural scientific research, in that it could investigate the laws of the bodily organization uninfluenced by interference from a spiritual manner of thinking. If one wishes to know according to what laws the reflected image comes into existence, one must give attention to the laws of the mirror. This determines how the beholder is reflected; it occurs in different ways depending on whether one has a plane, concave, or convex mirror. But the being of the person who is reflected is outside the mirror. One could thus see in the laws to be discovered through natural scientific research the reasons for the form of the empirical consciousness, and with these laws nothing should be mixed of what spiritual science has to say about the inner life of man's core of being. Within natural scientific research one will always rightly oppose the interference of purely spiritual points of view. It is natural that, in the area of this research, there is more sympathy with explanations which are given in a mechanistic way than with spiritual laws. A conception such as the following must be congenial to one who is at home in clear natural scientific conceptions: 'The fact of consciousness brought about by the stimulation of brain cells does not belong in a class essentially different from that of gravity connected with matter' (Moritz Benedikt).

In any case, such an explanation gives with exact methodology that which is conceivable for natural science. It is scientifically tenable, whereas the hypotheses of a direct control of the organic processes by psychic influences are scientifically untenable. But the idea previously given, fundamental from the point of view of the theory of knowledge, can see in the whole range of what can be established by natural science only arrangements which serve to reflect the real core of man's being. This core of being, however, is not to be located in the interior of the physical organization, but in the transcendental. Spiritual research would then be conceived as the way by which one attains knowledge of the real nature of that which is reflected. Obviously, the common basis of the laws of the physical organism and those of the supersensible would lie behind the antithesis, *being* and *mirror*. This, however, is certainly no disadvantage for the practice of the scientific method of approach from both directions. With the maintenance of the antithesis described, this method would, so to speak, flow in two currents, each reciprocally illuminating and clarifying the other. For it must be maintained that, in the physical organization, we are not dealing with a reflecting apparatus, in the absolute sense, independent of the supersensible. The reflecting apparatus must, after all, be considered as the product of the supersensible being who is mirrored in it. The relative reciprocal independence of the one and the other method of approach mentioned above must be supplemented by a third method coming to meet them, which enters into the depths of the problem and which is capable of beholding the synthesis of the sensible and the supersensible. The confluence of the two currents may be conceived as given through a possible further development of the life of the mind up to the intuitive cognition already described. Only within this cognition is that confluence superseded.

It may thus be asserted that epistemologically unbiased considerations open the way for rightly understood anthroposophy. For these lead to the conclusion that it is a theoretically understandable possibility that the core of man's being may have an existence free of the physical organization, and that the opinion of the ordinary consciousness—that the ego is to be considered a being absolutely within the body—is to be adjudged an inevitable illusion of the immediate life of the mind. The ego—with the whole of man's core of being—can be viewed as an entity which experiences its relationship to the objective world within that world itself, and receives its experiences as reflections in the form of impressions from the bodily organization. The separation of man's core of being from the bodily organization must, naturally, not be conceived spatially, but must be viewed as a relatively dynamic state of release. An apparent contradiction is then also resolved which might be discovered between what is here said and what has previously been said regarding the nature of sleep. In the waking state the human core of being is so fitted into the physical organization that it is reflected in this through the dynamic relationship to it; in the state of sleep the reflecting ceases. Since the ordinary consciousness, in the sense of the epistemological considerations here presented, is rendered possible only through the reflection (through the reflected representations), it ceases, therefore, during the state of sleep. The condition of mind of the spiritual researcher can be understood as one in which the illusion of the ordinary consciousness is overcome, and which gains a starting point in the life of soul from which it actually experiences the human core of being in free release from the bodily organization. All else which is then achieved through exercises is only a deeper delving into the transcendental, in which the ego of ordinary consciousness really exists although it is not aware of itself as within the transcendental.

Spiritual research is thus proved to be epistemologically conceivable. That it is conceivable will be admitted, naturally, only by one who can accept the view that the so-called critical theory of knowledge will be able to maintain its dogma of the impossibility of leaping over consciousness only so long as it fails to see through the illusion that the human core of being is enclosed within the bodily organization and receives impressions through the senses. I am aware that I have given only indications in outline in my epistemological exposition. Yet it may be possible to recognize from these indications that they are not isolated notions but grow out of a developed fundamental epistemological conception.

2. *Two Summaries of Essential Points from the Lecture in Bologna*

Theosophy and Modern Cultural Life

Of all the different viewpoints reflecting on the world, which were represented at the Fourth International Congress for Philosophy, many of our contemporaries will consider the theosophical one as one of the least scientific. One cannot be astonished about this fact. For much that initially appears at a time when it is considered fantastic and unfounded, becomes recognized in a later epoch, often even a self-evident truth. Even though theosophy, as characterized in a short lecture during this congress, is identified with spiritual streams that have often appeared in cultural evolution, it represents an absolutely new spiritual direction. It intends to open the door to a supersensible world. It will find this world not through mere speculative thinking, rather through real perception, which is just as accessible to the human soul as is perception by physical senses. Generally, a person thinks that perceptions of a spiritual kind that only appears to exceptionally gifted people in conditions of vision or ecstasy of the soul are not subject to scientific control. Therefore, one doesn't attach any more value to them beyond what they mean as the personal experiences of single individuals. Modern theosophy doesn't have anything in common with this kind of soul experience. It shows that in the human soul knowledge forces slumber which neither appear in normal everyday life nor external science. These forces can be awakened through meditation and energetic concentration of the inner sentient and willing life. In order to accomplish this, the soul must be able to cut itself off from all external impressions and everything the thinking preserves of them. Meditation is the soul's intensive dedication to imaginations, perceptions, and feelings so that instead of developing a consciousness of what these mean for the physical world, they turn out to be forces within the spiritual life that more or less illuminate the individuality and thus elicit from its depths powers of which the human being is not conscious in normal life. The effect of this inner immersion is such that through it the person is conscious of his own being as a spiritual reality, of which he otherwise has no perception. Before he engages in such exercises, he recognizes himself as a being who knows something about himself and the world through physical organs. After such exercises he knows that he can unfold a life in himself without his physical organs conveying it to him. He knows that he can separate himself spiritually from his physical body and that through this division he must not sink down into a condition of unconsciousness. He achieves not only such knowledge of himself, but also of a supersensible world, which is concealed from normal knowledge behind the physical-sense world and in which the true causes of the latter lie.

In this way, a person also learns to realize that as soul–spiritual being he descends from the heavenly world just as the physical being descends from terrestrial ancestors. Only he must sense that the soul–spiritual being from which he descends is *himself*, while his corporeal ancestors differ from him. This opens for him the prospect of repeated earth lives. Through real observation he learns to understand that human life consists truly of soul life in the physical body between birth and death, and thereafter a spiritual existence follows, which generally is of substantially longer duration than the physical. After this spiritual existence, a physical incorporation must follow again, and so forth, until the course of mortal incarnations is fulfilled when the earth reaches its culmination.

This idea of repeated earth lives (reincarnations) must of necessity seem paradoxical, even grotesque, to most of our contemporaries today. But it is just like the idea of Francesco Redi, who a few centuries ago—initially in opposition to his contemporaries—represented the idea that a life embryo cannot come into existence by combining lifeless material, but only as offspring of a similar type of living being. What appeared to people a few centuries ago as the fantastic idea of Francesco Redi is generally recognized truth today.

This is indicated in one of the many results of modern theosophy. The greatest misunderstandings come about when people think it is a renewal of Buddhism. It does *not* assume the same form as it has in the Orient. Even if Buddhism had never existed, the development of the higher knowledge forces characterized in the soul had to lead to the discovery of theosophical truths.

In its modern form, western theosophy doesn't want to be or found a religion, rather it hopes to expand science in the supersensible world. Thus, instead of being a religion, it is an instrument to deepen understanding of religious life. As such an instrument, it approaches Christianity; and it shows the depths of life prevailing in Christianity, which can only be found when a person draws near to it with a science of the supersensible. It shows how the founding of Christianity can only be grasped as a deed, which stems from a supersensible world and which has cast its rays into the physical–historical evolution of mankind. Especially thereby it is recognized how when a *person* completes his full earth life in repeated incorporations there appears the super-human, the divine nature of Christ. The Christ Being was for true supersensible observation only present *once* in a physical body. And since the Event on Golgotha He is connected with human evolution on earth. The epitome of supersensible observation consists of the fact that in the spiritual world Christ is recognized as the guiding force. The more the soul develops supersensible, cognitive powers, the nearer it comes to the Christ Being. theosophy does not disturb the religious belief of a Christian in any way, rather it is fixed as it is raised to a supersensible, scientific truth. Even when for normal knowledge the Being of Christianity can be doubtful for many people, it becomes a undeniable truth for spiritual scientific observation. Through the instrument of theosophy, truths contained in the Gospels can be seen in the right light.

For those, who have followed the theosophical spiritual direction since its founding in 1875 by the Theosophical Society, it can seem strange that the theosophical viewpoint is used here to represent this type of Christianity. That is because most people think theosophy's main teaching agrees with such oriental religious systems as Brahmanism or Buddhism. Of course, it is also correct to say that many representatives of theosophy still portray it in a manner which allows such opinion to appear justified. Nevertheless, it must be said that the initial founders of theosophy have not understood the Being of Christianity and that also today many important representatives of theosophy still do not understand it. Theosophy first had to reach a certain stage in order to recognize that Christianity not only represents an advancement compared to all preceding religious systems, rather it actually unites in itself the true aspects of all other religions when it is correctly understood.

Theosophy cannot be a religion as such; but it is a path to fully understanding religion, as it also is to the real understanding of nature and spirit. Therefore, at present due to these misconceptions, theosophical opponents are still increasing both on the part of religious collaborators as well as personalities adverse to religion. The first believe they could lose their religion through theosophy. By correctly immersing themselves in theosophy they will realize that true religiosity is just as little lost as the grandeur of nature appearances through scientific observation.

Others believe that theosophy must revert to blind belief. Through real knowledge of theosophy, they could convince themselves that the course of human history is not a series of errors, but a development of truth. They will come to the viewpoint that true science doesn't grasp the most beautiful flowers of human spiritual life—precisely the religious ones—by unveiling them as illusions, rather by unearthing their truth.

Whoever observes the development of souls in our time must find that in them lives a thirst for knowledge of the supersensible world. Normal sciences show amazing advancement. They have completely transformed our culture in a comparatively short time. They have provided solutions to questions about external life and will bring still much more in the future. Correctly observed, they have brought no solutions for soul life, but only raised new questions incessantly. No answer is given to such questions by traditional religious perceptions. One cannot argue here: These answers are available, only they are no longer found as solutions by many of our contemporaries.

That they are no longer found as such, is what essentially places before modern mankind new tasks for the inner life. When mankind grasps these tasks through spiritual science, then harmony can be created between the desires of souls advancing through modern life. If this grasping does not occur, then without solutions new questions must remain as burning thirst in the souls. However, questions that souls must pose without being able to attain answers means soul emptiness, soul unhappiness. Achieving answers to such questions means soul peace, soul strength, soul happiness. And modern mankind needs this if its splendid external culture should not become bereft of soul.

A Statement about Theosophy at the Fourth International Philosophy Conference

Dr Rudolf Steiner from Germany spoke about the psychological foundations of theosophy and its scientific justification within the Section for Philosophy of Religions. The speaker indicated that he had to represent a subject which in the broadest circles is still not viewed as scientific today. This is, however, quite understandable. For the spiritual direction in question is envisaged as a quite different type of knowledge than current, usual philosophical directions. People ask: What is the soul of man and in what way is it created? Theosophy, in the sense the speaker represents it, must say of the soul that it can rise above the so-called normal condition and thereby extend its knowledge forces beyond the area of sense and intellect to that of the supersensible. However, this neither means with such condition of the soul which in normal psychology is called subconscious or unconscious nor that of a vision, ecstasy, or something similar, but a condition achieved through strictest self-control of the personality. In order to arrive at this, the soul must endure strict, intimate exercises. It must penetrate itself with ideas, thoughts, and sensations that do not bear the usual character of external reality images, but which have a more symbolic character. The soul must now exclude from its life all sensual, conceptual and intellectual impressions and contents and in continual repetition be completely one with the symbolic imaginations characterized. From this results a quite definite experience, which insists that the soul grasps itself as inner reality, which rests in itself independent of the physical organization. Through this experience, a person knows that he really can live as soul independently of his body. The exercises must proceed from this point. The person must exclude the symbolic imaginations again from his soul life and only steer the inner sense to his own activity, to that activity through which he had experienced the symbols in himself. This exercise achieves a concentration of the soul independent from the body. The contents of the spiritual world flow into this inner life just like the sense content streams into the sense perceptions when eye and ear are directed to the external, physical world. Then new stages of knowledge are opened; the first, in which symbolic perceptions transform the soul life, can be called imaginative knowledge; the second, which starts to emerge when the symbols are eliminated again from consciousness, are called knowledge through inspiration. The speaker calls attention to how present scientific theories cannot accept such a described soul development, because from the beginning it places the human ego in the corporeal inner world. However, a knowledge theory of the future will acknowledge that the ego truly lies in the external spiritual world and the ordinary ego only mirrors its image in the bodily organization. Such a theory of knowledge will be able to be reconciled completely with theosophy.

In the short time allocated, a lively debate ensued after the speaker's accounts presented aphoristically. The well-known Platonist Dr W. Lutoslawski asked the speaker a number of questions. Through these it was mentioned that the soul exercises of the modern person—unlike those in olden times founded on physical isolation from the environment, on an extremely ascetic life and the like—place main emphasis on unfolding those spiritual–soul forces that lead to the isolation of consciousness within the person. To another question by Lutoslawski, the speaker remarked that methods of soul exercise, as they correspond to human beings of modern cultures, have been cultivated since the eleventh and twelfth centuries through a corresponding guide of spiritual life.

A further discussion speaker, Dr Stark, asked whether an objective criterion can be given for what a person finds as facts of the spiritual world after the corresponding preparation. The speaker answered that such a prepared soul is needed to research, to experience in the supersensible world, as has been described. However, when the facts of this world are disseminated in corresponding logical form, then the really impartial logic of the ordinary consciousness can decide about it and recognize it as correct. To a related question posed by the same discussion partner, Dr Steiner said the epoch is just beginning to appear in which the theosophy characterized will flow into spiritual–cultural life and be formulated into a recognized common property of human science.

Notes

1. The reader can find the Bologna Lecture, the knowledge of which enables a better understanding of my following remarks, in the little publication by Andreas Neider appearing in 2007 in the Rudolf Steiner Verlag in Dornach: *Das gespiegelte Ich. Der Bologna-Vortrag—die philosophischen Grundlagen der Anthroposophie.*
2. From the esoteric lesson of May 27, 1909, in Rudolf Steiner, *Esoteric Lessons,* Volume 1: 1904–1909 (GA 266/1).
3. About this, see further in S. O. Prokofieff, *Das Rätsel des menschlichen Ich. Eine anthroposophische Betrachtung*, Dornach 2010.
4. See Rudolf Steiner, *The Course of My Life*, Chapter I (GA 28).
5. A lecture entitled 'Paths to Knowledge of Higher Worlds' given on 26 November 1921, from the cycle *Self-Consciousness*, eight lectures, held in Christiania (GA 79).
6. Lecture from January 1, 1919, from the cycle *How Can Mankind Find the Christ Again? The Threefold Shadow-Existence of Our Time and the New Light of Christ* (GA 187).
7. In Chapter III, 'Thinking in the Service of Knowledge' (GA 4).
8. Chapter IX, 'The Idea of Freedom' (GA 4).
9. Letter to Josef Köck on January 13, 1881, published in *Letters*, Volume I (GA 38), not translated.
10. *The Course of My Life*, Chapter IV, italics Rudolf Steiner (GA 28).
11. See more detail about the Guardian of the Threshold in Rudolf Steiner, *Knowledge of the Higher Worlds and its Attainment*, Chapter 'The Guardian of the Threshold' (GA 10).
12. Lecture from August 27, 1912, from the cycle *Initiation, Eternity and the Passing Moment. From Spiritual Light and the Darkness of Life* (GA 138).
13. Lecture from November 26, 1921, from the cycle *Self-Consciousness*, eight lectures, held in Christiania (GA 79).
14. In the sense of Rudolf Steiner's book *Theosophy* (GA 9) the words 'spiritual world' correspond to the four lower areas of spirit land and the phrase 'super-spiritual world' to the three upper regions.
15. Lecture from August 30, 1913, from the cycle *Secrets of the Threshold* (GA 147).
16. Rudolf Steiner describes this meeting with Christ in Intuition from another point of view in his book *Occult Science—an Outline*, at the end of the chapter 'Knowledge of the Higher Worlds (through Initiation)' (GA 13).
17. See further regarding Rudolf Steiner's path to the new Christ consciousness in S. O. Prokofieff, *The Appearance of Christ in the Etheric. Spiritual-Scientific Aspects of the Second Coming*, chapter 7, 'The Supersensible Mystery of

Golgotha and Rudolf Steiner's Initiation', English edition Temple Lodge 2012.

18. *The Course of My Life*, chapter XXVI (GA 28).
19. Here one must fundamentally distinguish the Eastern idea of reincarnation (which conceives of repeated earthly lives as a kind of circular movement, which has neither beginning nor end and therefore must be abandoned with all the means accessible to the soul) from the understanding of reincarnation in anthroposophy. For more information about this, see Rudolf Steiner *Theosophy*, chapter 'Reincarnation of the Spirit and Destiny (Reincarnation and Karma)' (GA 9).
20. Italics by Rudolf Steiner.
21. Essay from 9 November, 1924. 'Michael's Mission in the Cosmic Age of Human Freedom', from the book *Anthroposophical Leading Thoughts. The Anthroposophical Path of Knowledge—The Michael Mystery* (GA 26).